Branch Lines of East 1

Volume Two

Woodhall Junction
to Horncastle

A. J. Ludlam

Published by the
Lincolnshire Wolds Railway Society

LWRS
PUBLICATIONS

Parker class N5 0-6-2T No 69327, of Lincoln shed, with the
4.05 pm "school train" to Woodhall Junction in 1951. *J. Cupit.*

LONG HALF-DAY AT THE SEASIDE.

JACKSON & SON'S

ANNUAL EXCURSION TO

SKEGNESS

. AND .

BOSTON

SPECIAL THROUGH TRAIN

Wednesday, July 4th, 1906.

Ample accomodation provided. Two trains guaranteed.

Early application for reserved compartments requested.

HORNCASTLE	....	....	....	12.40
WOODHALL SPA	....	....	....	12.50
KIRKSTEAD	....	....	....	12.55
TATTERSHALL	....	....	...	1.4

1/9

CHILDREN UNDER 12 HALF-PRICE.

Returning from Skegness at 7.30 and 8.30 p.m.

THE HORNCASTLE TOWN AND VOLUNTEER BAND.

(under the conductorship of Mr. F. Blyth, Bandmaster), will accompany the trip, and play Selections in the Pavilion Gardens after tea.

All goods to the amount of £1 and upwards, purchased for cash between June 1st and July 4th, 1906, will entitle the purchaser to a

Free Ticket.

Paid-up Members of the Clothing Club Free.

TICKETS for the Trip may be had of Messrs. Jackson & Son, North Street, at any time, and at the Railway Stations on the day of Trip.

A SPECIAL MEAT TEA

Will be provided in the Pavilion. Tickets 1s. each.

W. K. Morton, & Sons, Ltd., Printers. Horncastle.   86706

ISBN 978-0-9926762-6-1

The Lincolnshire Wolds Railway Society would like to thank Alf Ludlam and Phil Eldridge for giving their time to compile this publication, to Woodhall Spa Cottage Museum, The Museum of Lincolnshire Life, David Enefer, Marjorie Cook, Adam Cartwright, Michael Stewart and Leyland Penn for their contributions and to Allinson Print & Supplies for their support with the project.

Printed by Allinson Print & Supplies, Allinson House, Lincoln Way, Fairfield Industrial Estate, Louth, Lincolnshire LN11 0LS

Issue 1. June 2015.

CONTENTS

Some staff and a customer at the entrance to Horncastle station in the 1920s.

The original swing bridge over the Witham at Kirkstead Junction.

Woodhall Spa station and Broadway, with engine No 292 on a branch train for Kirkstead Junction in 1909.

INTRODUCTION

Horncastle is a pleasant market town, situated where the Lincolnshire Wolds meet the fens. In Roman times it was a fortress called Bonovallum, meaning "the walled place on the Bain". The town stands on the banks of the rivers Bain and Waring, their meeting forms a horn-like tongue of land, from which the town takes its name.

In the autumn of 1643 the Royalists were besieging Hull and the Parliamentarians were marching from Boston to relieve the city. Fairfax occupied Horncastle for the Parliamentarians, but troops of cavaliers and foot soldiers were on their way from Lincoln to halt the advance. They organised their troops on high ground between Horncastle and Spilsby, near the hamlet of Winceby. In the first charge Cromwell had his horse shot from under him, but he remounted and led a second charge, which sent the Royalists scattering through Horncastle and Lincoln, only drawing rein when they reached Newark. The battle confirmed Cromwell's status and Lincolnshire as a Parliamentary county.

With a population of around 2,000 at the end of the 18th century, most of which was restricted to within a ten-mile radius of the town, due to poor roads, the situation needed to change if the town was to develop.

Sir Joseph Banks, from nearby Revesby Abbey, was responsible for much of the change. The Horncastle Canal opened in 1802; three years later the open field

A train approaches Woodhall Spa station over the level crossing bound for Horncastle on a snow-covered winter's day. *Cottage Museum Collection.*

system had gone and the fields were enclosed, thus releasing land for housing and industrial development. The population began to increase rapidly. The arrival of the canal was the beginning of Horncastle's development as a thriving Victorian town, celebrated for its great horse fair, once the biggest in the land.

John Parkinson was born near Horncastle in 1772. He sank a shaft looking for coal near Woodhall in 1811. No coal was found and the shaft flooded. It was the Lord of Woodhall Manor, Thomas Hotchkin, who discovered the bromo-iodine rich waters contained in the shaft benefitted his gout. He opened the original Bath and Pump House in 1838. By the 1840s over two thousand people a year were being treated. With the advent of the railway numbers increased dramatically.

In the early 1880s Woodhall Spa was comprised of the Spa Baths, the Victoria Hotel, St Andrews Church and less than ten houses. London architect Richard Adolphus Carne was commissioned to plan a small garden city with a tree-lined broadway and a shopping area. He came and lived in the Royal Hydro Hotel complex he had designed.

The Alexandra Hospital was built in 1890 and the Home for Gentlewomen in 1894. The golf course opened a year later. In 1898 Woodhall Spa became an Urban District and by the end of the century there were over a hundred houses. The population of just under a thousand increased to over sixteen hundred by 1921.

Petwood was built by Grace Maple, daughter of Sir John Blundell Maple, of furniture fame. It was her country house in her 'pet wood' near the Spa Baths. In 1910 Grace married Captain Archibald Weigall. They entertained on a vast scale, with many notable guests, including Royalty, Lady Louis Mountbatten and Sir Donald Campbell. Petwood became a hotel in 1933 and was taken over by the RAF from 1943 to 45 and became the officers' mess of 617 Squadron, the 'Dam Busters'. *Cottage Museum Collection.*

In 1848 the Great Northern Railway (GNR) built a railway between Boston and Lincoln, which became known as the Loop Line. Three years later it built a coal wharf and warehouse at Dogdyke, at the entrance to the Horncastle Canal. Coal and other goods were offloaded from trains, transferred to barges and carried by canal to Horncastle, using the boats of George Gilliott. The resultant increase in canal traffic saw the GNR paying £1,677 in canal tolls in 1852. However, by 1853 these had fallen to £1,254.

The decrease was, no doubt, due to the formation of a company to promote the construction of a railway line from Horncastle to Kirkstead, on the Boston-Lincoln line. Under the leadership of Sir Henry Dymoke, a former chairman of the canal company, J. Banks-Stanhope and S. Sketchley, the company was in a position, by the end of the year, to approach the GNR to try and establish terms by which that company would work the line for the Horncastle Railway Company (HRC). A suitable agreement was drawn up based upon the "Estimates of Working Expenses", given to the HRC in a letter from Seymour Clarke, General Manager of the GNR. This was based on two trains a day each way working over the 7½ mile branch line, one engine doing all the work, plus staff wages, maintenance, ticket sales etc. Clarke concluded "I contemplate no charge being made for the use of Kirkstead station. All alterations at Kirkstead to be paid for by the HRC, including the signal station

Horncastle station frontage on 10th July, 1954. A fine Georgian-style building, intended to fit in with the towns architectural style. The single-storied section at the far end was a 1900 addition.

at the Kirkstead Junction and a small engine house and carriage shed". The terms of Clarke's letter were accepted by the HRC and the "Horncastle & Kirkstead Junction Railway" Bill was presented to Parliament.

Opposition to the railway was strong and mainly took the form of broadsheets, the railway promoters replied using the same method. A valid point was made in a broadsheet published under the name "Fairplay", "As regards the advantage this Rail will make to the Trade of Horncastle - can you for a moment suppose that its trading establishments, such as Grocers, Ironmongers, Linen drapers, Chemists etc are of that quality to tempt parties living at a distance, say Lincoln or Boston, to come to Horncastle by rail to make their purchases? Or don't you think it more probable that the few independent people living in Horncastle, and neighbourhood, would take advantage of the Rail to go to Boston and Lincoln, where there are most certainly a better, larger and cheaper assortment of goods for sale, to make their purchases instead of Horncastle? How would this benefit the town? Ask the tradesmen of Alford, Market Rasen, or any other small market town, how much their Rail has benefitted, or injured them. The fact is that the Rail would be for the benefit of Boston and Lincoln and damage the trade in Horncastle."

These accusations were borne out to a degree. The cheap fares charged by the railway did encourage people to shop out-of-town in Boston and Lincoln, and, bringing into the town cheap manufactured goods, caused the disappearance of small industries and skilled jobs.

Despite the strong opposition the Bill passed through Parliament and was given Royal Assent on 10th July, 1854. The HRC had the power to raise £48,000 capital and had a borrowing capacity of £13,000. By early August it was reported that three quarters of the capital shares had been taken up.

The first Ordinary General Meeting of the Company was held at the Bull Hotel, Horncastle, on 21st September, 1854. Thomas Brassey had purchased £15,000 in shares in the company, on the understanding that he would be given the contract to build the line.

In comparison with other Lincolnshire branch lines, the Horncastle was unique in two regards. Firstly, it continued to make a profit during its lifetime as an independent company, until its takeover by the London & North Eastern Railway (LNER) in 1923. Secondly, as a result, it remained in the control of the parent company until that time.

The ferry across the River Witham at Kirkstead prior to its closure in 1891. There is plenty of activity on the river, a Boston to Lincoln passenger train stands in the station platform.

Horncastle terminus. Class N5 0-6-2T No 69327 has marshalled the wagons for the 6.00 pm goods train and taken its place at the head of the 4.05 pm passenger train to Woodhall Junction. This view from the signal box shows the water tank and water column on the left. *J. Cupit.*

A special outing, possibly a Sunday School party, at Horncastle station in 1913.

Locomotive No 729 moves over the level-crossing at Woodhall Spa station in 1916. All that remains now is the row of shops in Broadway.

CONSTRUCTION OF THE LINE

Because of the severe winter of 1854/55 work could not begin on the construction of the line until March 1855. At Horncastle Mr Darby's tannery was demolished to make way for the station. During March and April steady progress was made on the line and, by May, the railway was within three miles of Horncastle. The "Lincolnshire Chronicle" strongly disapproved of Sunday afternoon sightseers who visited the workings, and reported, "At present the works are a source of great annoyance to some farmers as they attract a number of idle youths who spend their Sundays "racing, jumping and breaking down fences". The "Chronicle" also raised a disapproving eyebrow to the instigation of Sunday working in order to complete the line by the 7th August.

The line was completed during the second week in August, opening celebrations were planned for the 11th. The day before the official opening, Colonel Wynne inspected the line and refused to pass it fit for passenger travel as heavy rain had caused the soil on an embankment to settle unevenly.

The despondency of the HRC officers was not, however, reflected in the town itself. Great celebrations took place on the appointed day, with flags, bunting and

A GNR 0-4-2 tender engine leaves Woodhall Spa with a train for Horncastle prior to 1923.
Cottage Museum Collection.

four triumphal arches, as well as much feasting and a firework display to end the day.

The contractors worked hard to get the line ready for the Horncastle fair on 17th August, Colonel Wynne again inspected the line and pronounced it fit for traffic. The line ran single for 7 miles 28 chains and earthworks were light, with only one overbridge. The line left Kirkstead Junction by a gentle curve and proceeded north towards Woodhall Spa. It climbed across Thornton Moor, after which it entered a small cutting and on through a low spur of the Lincolnshire Wolds, passing under the Kirkstead-Horncastle road at Martin's Bridge. From here it ran alongside the canal towards Horncastle station.

A view from the footbridge at Woodhall Spa station in the direction of Woodhall Junction. The stationmaster's house is to the right of the crossing gates. *Cottage Museum Collection.*

The original station at Woodhall Spa with a train for Horncastle at the platform. The stationmaster's house is on the left. *Cottage Museum Collection.*

Humpherson & Company's shop in Tattershall Road with an interesting variety of wheeled vehicles on display. To the right of the group of men is the weighbridge office standing in the goods yard at Woodhall Spa. *Cottage Museum Collection.*

(Above) The Woodhall Spa stationmaster and his staff in LNER days. Unfortunately we have no names. *Cottage Museum Collection.*

(Left) Station staff and a small boy near the cast-iron gent's urinal at Woodhall Junction station. *Cottage Museum Collection.*

Woodhall Spa station looking toward Woodhall Junction in the 1950s. No doubt the signalman here was pretty fit, as he had to run from the signal box to open and close the crossing gates. *D. Thomson.*

The Broadway, Woodhall Spa, onto which backed the station buildings.

The crew of class C2 4-4-2 await the "right away" from Woodhall Junction with a Skegness bound passenger train in 1930. *J. Wrottesley.*

Large numbers of people and horses arrived at Horncastle by rail for the annual Horse Fair, which was the railways first great success. The next most crucial test was whether the railway was capable of generating enough revenue through the autumn and winter to justify its existence.

With the advent of the railway there was a sharp drop in the passenger traffic on the Horncastle Canal, and, in 1855, the canal company reduced the tolls in an effort to compete. However, traffic continued to decline over the next twenty years; takings of £896 in 1859 had fallen to £148 by 1879.

Fortune was against the canal company in 1855, when a severe frost in December froze the canal and suspended traffic on it. Local coal merchants began to realise the value of the railway and started ordering their coal by rail. The price of coal in Horncastle dropped to an average of 13s 6d (67$\frac{1}{2}$p) per ton, only the previous year it had been 17s 6d (87$\frac{1}{2}$p).

After years of struggling against financial difficulties the canal was officially declared defunct as from 23rd September, 1889, by the Board of Trade (Railway Department). Further encouragement to use the railway came from the introduction of cheap excursions to London, for 6 shillings return, in October 1855. The October figures were excellent - 2,580 quarters of grain had been despatched from Horncastle and 500 tons of goods received. 4,156 sheep, 298 head of cattle, 48 horses, 35 pigs and 91 calves had been sent out. Passenger figures showed 3,200 persons carried.

Horncastle station staff with stationmaster Everleigh in the centre.

During the winter of 1855 shares in the HRC rose considerably and consequently it was impossible to buy them. By September 1856 a dividend of 3s (15p) per share was announced. The shares rose again in 1857 and a dividend of 4s 6d (22½p) was paid. By 1876 the HRC was paying a dividend of 8s 3d (41p) per share. The sponsors of the HRC had proved that the town could support the line and, in 1876, the old 1855 agreement with the GNR was renewed on its original terms.

In 1890 the Board of Trade asked the HRC to improve the line. Thinking it might have problems raising the capital the company's directors offered to sell the line to the GNR for £18 per £10 share. The GNR was unable to meet the price and instead offered the HRC a seven-year loan at 4% interest. The rest of the capital was raised by the HRC and its independence retained.

During World War 1 the company came under the control of the Railway Executive Committee and a fixed dividend of 6% was paid for the duration of the war. Afterwards things returned to normal until the 1923 grouping, at which the GNR became part of the London & North Eastern Railway (LNER). From its inception the HRC had been profitable, rarely paying dividends of less than 6%.

Horncastle station had a single platform and a train shed over the passenger line. There was a run round loop and a short bay to the east. There were two additional goods roads to the west, one of them connected to the run round loop by the wagon turntable, the other was a dead end serving the cattle pens.

Horncastle from the station throat shows the area occupied by the railway from the goods loading dock, with its 5-ton crane, on the left to the coal yard on the right. *J. Cupit.*

Horncastle signal box. The Regulations of Railways Act of 1869 provided the inspections for the completion of Interlocking on the GNR. The contract for resignalling at Horncastle was given to the Railway Signal Company. The resulting work included this 25-lever box, which was brought into use on 21st January, 1891.

The goods shed stood beyond the end of the station platform, near the buffer stops. It was served by a wagon turntable, operated by a shunting horse, which was stabled at the far end of the yard near the signal box. The line which served the goods shed actually crossed the passenger line on the level, an unusual arrangement. The platform end, near the goods shed, ended in a flight of steps rather than the usual slope. In a sense this was illegal under Board of Trade regulations, but as this end of the terminus was regarded as a goods area the usual regulations regarding passenger facilities did not apply.

Improvements were carried out at Horncastle in 1874 when the platform was lengthened. Sidings serving Sutcliffe's Malt Kiln and Harrisons Corn Mill and coal drops were provided for, among others, Harrisons, Carter & White and Lancaster. Petrol was delivered to Ashchurch's until the branch closed.

Lincoln-based class B1 4-6-0 No 61281 arrives at Woodhall Junction with the 9.00 am Lincoln to Skegness passenger train on 29th April, 1954. On the opposite platform, behind the lamp, stands the cast iron gent's urinal, which is now preserved at the Museum of Lincolnshire Life, in Lincoln. *R. M. Casserley.*

Horncastle station in the 1950s, the lighter brickwork on the station wall indicates where the former train shed was located. *D. Thompson.*

Class A5 4-6-2T No 69804 stands in the platform at Horncastle with the afternoon passenger service to Woodhall Junction.

WOODHALL SPA

The only intermediate station on the branch was at Woodhall Spa. In 1888 the HRC bought land at Woodhall Spa to facilitate the building of a new station. This included a 340-yard passing loop, two platforms, a new waiting room, booking hall and bookshop. A platform canopy on the south side, a new signal box on the north platform and a footbridge completed the improvements. It was the emergence of

Woodhall Spa as a health resort, which found the original single platform and waiting room severely wanting. The Spa's boom was between 1880 and 1914, but its decline as a Spa coincided with its emergence as a golfing centre, attracting many visitors during the 1920s and 30s. Coal drops were provided at Woodhall Spa, and the siding held twelve wagons. The cost of the 1888 improvements totalled £6,112, 16s, and 2d.

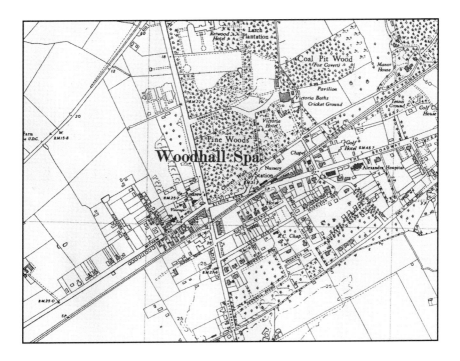

A class C12 4-4-2T stands in the platform at Horncastle with its train under the train shed in the 1930s. The top of the yard crane and the loading gauge can be seen over the vans alongside the loading dock on the left. *J. Wrottesley.*

Class N5 0-6-2T No 69253 awaits departure from Woodhall Junction station with a Horncastle train in April 1953. No 69253 was built for the GCR by Beyer, Peacock & Co. in August 1893 and was finally withdrawn in November 1955. *R. K. Blencowe.*

THE HORNCASTLE RAILWAY.
DIVIDEND DECLARED 22nd MARCH, 1916.

Horncastle, 22nd March, 1916.

Madam,

I beg to annex a Draft, No. *72*, the balance of the Dividend on your shares in this Railway, for the year ending 31st December, 1915, after deducting the Interim Dividend paid 22nd September last, viz :

	£	s.	d.	£	s.	d.
....*33*....Shares at 6/- per share	*10*	*10*	*0*			
Less Income Tax at 3/3 per £	*1*	*14*	*1*	*8*	*15*	*11*

I am, Madam,

Your obedient Servant,

H. TWEED

Secretary.

I hereby certify that the Income Tax deducted from the amount of this Warrant has been, or will be, paid over by the said Company to the proper Officer for the receipt of Taxes.

H. TWEED, Secretary.

Mrs S. E. Fletcher —

Woodhall Junction, looking towards Boston from the road bridge. Everything is beginning to look run down and in need of a coat of paint in this late view. *M. Cook.*

21

AUGUST BANK HOLIDAY
TO
LANGRICK DOGDYKE
TATTERSHALL
WOODHALL JCN.
WOODHALL SPA
HORNCASTLE

DAY EXCURSION TICKETS

MONDAY, 1st AUGUST

FROM	DEPARTURE TIMES			RETURN FARES—THIRD CLASS					
				LANG-RICK	DOG-DYKE	TATTER-SHALL	WOOD-HALL JCN.	WOOD-HALL SPA	HORN-CASTLE
	a.m.	p.m.	p.m.	s. d.	s. d.	s. d.	s. d.	s. d.	s. d.
Boston ...	7 55	12 12	3 25	8	1 5	1 6	2 0	2 0	2 0
Langrick ...	8 4	12 21	3 34	—	—	—	1 5	1 7	2 0
Dogdyke...	8 14	12 31	3 44	—	—	—	—	9	1 6
Tattershall	8 17	12 34	3 47	—	—	—	—	9	1 5

Returning same day by any Ordinary Train or by Special Train leaving
Horncastle 7-50 p.m.   Woodhall Spa 8-2 p.m.   Woodhall Jcn. 8-20 p.m.
Tattershall 8-29 p.m.   Dogdyke 8-32 p.m.   Langrick 8.44 p.m.
due Boston 8-53 p.m.

It will assist the Railway Company in making arrangements FOR YOUR COMFORT if you
TAKE TICKETS IN ADVANCE

TICKETS CAN BE OBTAINED IN ADVANCE AT THE STATIONS

FOR CONDITIONS OF ISSUE SEE OVER

THE HOLIDAY HANDBOOK
At L·N·E·R Stations, Offices and Agencies— 6d.

London, July, 1932   (E.T. and O.T.)   (No. 2952)

L·N·E·R
2,000

Lincolnshire Chronicle & Leader, Printers, Lincoln

Left: The canopy covering the main and bay platforms at Woodhall Junction on March 1st, 1980.
A. Cartwright.

Above: A view of the old trackbed at Thornton Crossing with the canal to the right. This is now part of the Viking Way.
P. Eldridge.

Left: The Warehouse that stood in Horncastle station yard seen here in 1982.
A. J. Ludlam.

Above: Woodhall Junction station today.
P. Eldridge

Left: Horncastle station approach and elegant building on 1st April, 1981. *A. Cartwright.*

Below left: The cast iron gent's urinal at Woodhall Junction station, built in Glasgow in the 1880s.

Below right: The same urinal, now preserved at the Museum of Lincolnshire Life in Lincoln.
Museum of Lincolnshire Life.

KIRKSTEAD JUNCTION

At Kirkstead Junction the station buildings were of the "Italianate" style used along the Boston-Lincoln line. The tall three-storey tower had a particularly large chimney and overhanging roof, while the windows had semi-circular arches.

The station was altered for the opening of the Horncastle branch in 1855. The junction here faced the wrong way. A short bay platform was built to accommodate Horncastle trains, on the up side. The branch engine would propel its train out of the platform for some distance before reversal was affected, on a short spur alongside the main line. Trains could then enter the branch facing the right way.

A large canopy, supported by wooden pillars, was provided on the up platform serving the Boston trains and the bay platform. On the down side a small canopy was attached to a wooden waiting shelter, with its back to the River Witham. Alongside stood an ornate cast-iron gents urinal, a large square water tank stood atop a brick base, between the platform and the signal box. There was a level crossing to the north of the station, the gates operated by a gateman, acting upon bell codes received from the signal box. When the ferry crossed the Witham at Kirkstead the gateman took the toll money from ferry passengers. The signal box at Kirkstead was worked on a three-shift system.

After the closure of the ferry in 1891 a bridge was built across the Witham. Farmers with goods, cows and sheep would pay a toll to cross the bridge, the tolls

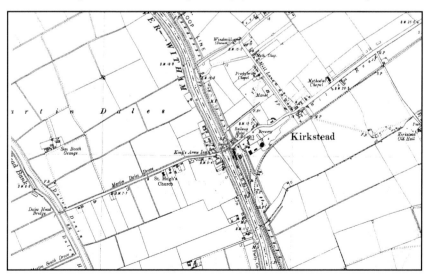

going to the station because the GNR owned the bridge.

The name Kirkstead Junction was changed to Woodhall Junction in 1922, largely due to the efforts of Sir Archibald Weigall, who lived at Petwood in Woodhall Spa, to popularise the Spa as a golfing resort.

Mr Winter was the gateman at Woodhall Junction, he enjoyed tending the garden at the gatehouse, the station often won the competition for the best-kept station garden, the diplomas were hung in the waiting room. Mr Osborn, the stationmaster, was followed by Mr Pleasance, father of the actor Donald Pleasance.

Mr Winter's daughter, Gladys recalled. "the wages were low but there were perks for working on the railway. There was a free market pass and my mother and I would go to Boston on Wednesday or Lincoln on Fridays. There was also the 'PT' (privilege ticket), this was about a third of the normal fare, with which we could travel to London or up to Elgin in Scotland. For years my parents had a short holiday in Aberdeen, because they could get there for almost nothing".

An engineering department motor trolley was kept here. Engineer gangers were Messrs Gray and Howard and patrolmen Messrs White and Townell.

Woodhall Junction station looking toward Lincoln in the 1950s. The impressive station nameboard is noteworthy. *D. Thompson.*

The "small engine shed and carriage shed" at Kirkstead, proposed in Seymour Clarke's original letter to the HRC, never materialised. An engine shed was built at Horncastle about which little is known, but it is likely to have been about 65ft x 20ft in area. Coaling was carried out from a wagon and water was stored in a 7,500 gallon tank near the signal box. Engines were likely to have been 0-4-2T, 0-4-4T and 2-4-0s supplied by Boston shed.

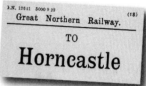

Engines were changed over using the 6.25 am Boston to Kirkstead goods return. Mr Martin, of Woodhall Spa, who worked on the branch all his life, was positive that an engine was shedded at Horncastle between 1920 and 1922 with the sole purpose of working the branch. He recalled a Stirling 0-4-2 tender engine, No 25A, the driver Harry Curtis and his fireman and cleaner Wright both lived in Horncastle.

The GNR timetable for 1882 shows the branch operating mixed trains of passenger, goods and coal at all times, except the 2.45 pm goods and coal only, which ran from Kirkstead on Tuesdays, Thursdays and Saturdays "when required". The same arrangement applied to the 3.00 pm from Horncastle. Departures from Horncastle were at 6.40, 8.22 and 9.45 am (WO), 12.00, 2.00 and 5.47 pm. Return journeys left Kirkstead at 7.12, 9.00 (ThX), 9.14 (TO), 10.13 (WO) and 10.58 am, 1.19, 4.15 and the last train at 6.35 pm, which arrived at Horncastle at 6.58 pm.

There is no doubt that, after 1923, engines were supplied daily from Boston shed, except for an engine from Lincoln that worked the goods.

Passengers on the Horncastle branch were conveyed in an articulated set numbered 44161/2, which had been formed from the carriage units of GNR steam rail motors No's 5 and 6. The original bogies were retained at the outer ends and a shared bogie was provided in the middle. The first coach provided third-class accommodation, whilst the second had a first-class smoking compartment and a third-class coupé. The length of the set was 110ft 7ins over the buffers. The coaches were originally built by the Birmingham Carriage & Wagon Co Ltd and had semi-elliptical roofs. The engine portions of the railcars were scrapped in 1927 and No's 44161/2 arrived on the branch soon afterwards. The set survived the closure of the branch to passenger traffic in 1954, finally being scrapped in 1959.

Class A5 4-6-2T No 69804 of Lincoln shed stands in the bay platform at Woodhall Junction with a passenger train for Horncastle. Built for the GCR in May 1911, No 69804 was withdrawn in April 1958.

Class N5 0-6-2T No 69311, a unique member of the class because of its extended side-tanks. The gap in the tank allows access to the motion. The tanks and bunker were extended in 1915 to allow the engine to carry an extra 640 gallons of water and one ton of coal in order to work the shuttle service between Chester and Shotton, their being no water column at Shotton. When shedded at Lincoln, as well as working the Horncastle branch, it was used on station pilot duties, and was withdrawn in January 1957.

THE THROUGH COACH

After World War 1 Horncastle was served by a connection on the 3.00 pm from Kings Cross to Cromer express. A coach was attached to the front of the train at Kings Cross. Arriving at Peterborough the coach would be picked up by the 4.40 pm slow train which would draw out of the bay platform and back onto the Cromer train to attach the Horncastle coach. The coach would be detached at Kirkstead and arrive at Horncastle at 6.50 pm.

In June 1922 the daily Horncastle through coach was attached to the 4.00 pm from Kings Cross with a corresponding return, which ran throughout the year. This carriage was worked with the Grimsby portion of the train and worked to and from Boston. The through coach was left overnight at Horncastle. Next morning a parcels train left Boston at 6.25 am, the engine returned, arriving at Boston at 10.16 am with the through coach, which was attached to the up express. This through coach was advertised until 1932. After this time a connecting service between Boston and Horncastle operated. The through carriage was reinstated on the 4.00 pm, Fridays and Saturdays only in the summer of 1936/37 with up workings on Mondays and Saturdays.

The running of the through coaches was almost certainly connected with the great efforts being made to popularize Woodhall Spa as a holiday resort and golfing centre, during the 1920s. The campaign was orchestrated by Sir Archibald Weigall, the local MP. Frequent passengers on the through coach were Queen Alexandra and her daughter Princess Helena Victoria, who stayed with Sir Archibald at Petwood.

The station at Woodhall Spa looking towards Horncastle. The Broadway is to the right and the stationmaster's house to the left. *Cottage Museum Collection.*

Woodhall Spa station looking towards Woodhall Junction on 28th April, 1954. The unusual pattern of the fencing is echoed on the back wall of the waiting shelter. *H. C. Casserley.*

Class N5 0-6-2T No 69275 arriving at Horncastle station from Woodhall Junction on 14th March, 1952. *J. F. Oxley.*

A British Railways class J6 0-6-0 No 64244 works a train to Horncastle past the corrugated iron bungalow that was home to photographer John Wield, now the Cottage Museum. *Cottage Museum Collection.*

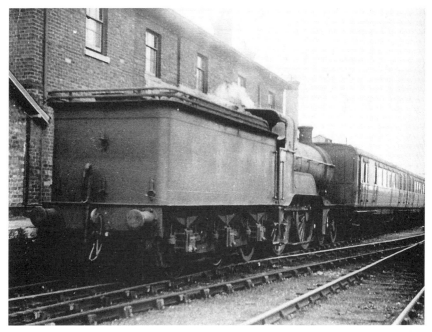

A class D2 4-4-0 prepares to run round the Horncastle set for the return trip to Woodhall Junction. *S. Priestley.*

The elegant footbridge at Woodhall Spa station with the Broadway and the Eagle Lodge Hotel beyond. Originally known as Eagle House when built by Charles Blyton in the mid-1870s. *Cottage Museum Collection.*

A GNR tender engine pulls an interesting bird-cage carriage near Woodhall Spa station. The glassed area at the top of the carriage allowed the guard to look along the length of the train. *Cottage Museum Collection.*

G. H. DALES, STATIONMASTER

The station records kept by Mr G. H. Dales, who was stationmaster at Horncastle from 1906 until the late 20s, recorded that Easter 1906 saw 262 passengers arriving at Horncastle on Thursday 12th April, one extra coach being required on the branch train. On Good Friday, 13th April, 19 passengers booked for Lincoln, 215 for Skegness, 6 for Boston and 11 for Woodhall Spa. A six-coach train was used and worked through to Lincoln. On Bank Holiday Monday 257 passengers booked for Skegness and 28 for Woodhall Spa. The train was made up of seven coaches. Mr Dales noted, "Weather exceptionally fine during the whole holiday, if the same next year we should be prepared with ten vehicles for the special". A similar note regarding the length of trains also followed the entry for the 8th July, when 1,001 passengers were carried in two trains. "The trains were uncomfortably full and next year each train should consist of fourteen coaches each".

Jackson's Excursions to Skegness were, for many years, an annual event. On 4th July, 1906, 1037 passengers made the journey, the records state, "Both trains were full, Kirkstead had to attach a carriage on the second train. One train was made up of fourteen coaches, the other of twelve."

The Newmarket Horse Sales, in December, saw six mares, the property of Mr Taylor-Sharp, loaded in two horse boxes on the 11.00 am train to Boston and from there on by a special to Newmarket. Two days later thirty-six horses from Mr Elsey, were loaded into thirteen horse boxes on the 9.50 am to Boston and thence to Newmarket. Also attached to the train, on each occasion, was a lavatory compo coach to work through, for the uses of Messrs Taylor-Sharp and Elsey.

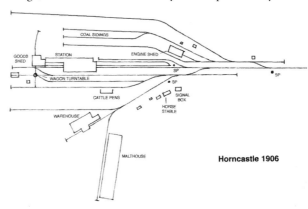

Horncastle 1906

Class J6 0-6-0 No 64199 with a Railway Correspondence and Travel Society Special at Horncastle on 16th May, 1954. The photo was taken from the signal box and shows the station area and the coal drops on the right. *Real Photographs Co.*

Class N5 0-6-2T No 69253 at Horncastle station with a train from Woodhall Junction.

The unique class N5 0-6-2T No 9311 runs round its train at Horncastle in 1947. *J. Kite.*

THE LINE AT WORK

The cattle and sheep fairs and markets meant considerable work and revenue for the railway, for example the loadings for the First Spring Market, 29th March, 1906, are shown in the table below.

It was the job of the platelayers based at Horncastle to wash out the cattle pens and for this they were issued with clogs, which replaced their own boots. At the time of the sheep fairs special trains were put on to transport the animals from Horncastle. As many as seven engines at a time were at Horncastle on such occasions, and, in the early 1900s, thirty trains a day were often seen on the branch at the time of the Thursday Sheep Fairs.

An entry in "Morton's Almanac" of 1921 concerned the retirement of Charlie Cook, of 54 Prospect Street,

FIRST DAY	
242 cattle	26 cattle wagons
3,072 sheep	150 high-sided wagons
TOTAL 3,314	176
SECOND DAY	
No cattle	1 cattle wagon
2,643 sheep	129 high-sided wagons
73 sheep	3 cattle wagons
TOTAL 2,716	134
GROSS 6,030	309

Horncastle, after 47 years service, it gave the names of several stationmasters at Horncastle: "Mr Charles Joseph Cook, who retired on Saturday 10th July, 1920, after 47 years service at Horncastle GNR station. Mr Cook was born at Mavis Enderby on 17th September, 1848, and after several years of working on the land entered the service of the GNR Company on 11th May, 1870, being transferred to Horncastle as a shunter three years later. For 37 out of the 47 years he had been at Horncastle he had held the position of foreman, under Mr. G. Everleigh. Upon Mr Everleigh's retirement Mr Clark was appointed stationmaster for a few years, before being transferred to Bourne. Following Mr Ridout, who was stationmaster for a short while, G. H. Dales, the present incumbent, came from Skegness to take up the duties. It is significant that during the last 25 years of his service Mr Cook has not been absent from his work for a single day through sickness".

For the last ten years before the withdrawal of the passenger services British Railways maintained a very simple timetable with the line not operating on Sundays. The six day service began with the 6.25 am three coach from Boston to Woodhall Junction. Running tender first this was latterly hauled by a class A5 4-6-2T or a class J6 0-6-0. This train included the Horncastle parcels van and

Class N5 0-6-2T No 69253 has propelled its train into the bay platform at Woodhall Junction on 7th April, 1953. A wicker basket is off-loaded whilst the crew relaxes after the afternoon journey from Horncastle. *J. Bonser.*

formed the 7.15 am to Horncastle. Returning to the Junction it connected with the Lincoln-Skegness and Boston to Lincoln trains at approximately 8.15 am. A second trip to Horncastle and back connected with the Lincoln to Skegness and the Skegness to Lincoln trains, before forming the 9.50 am from Woodhall Junction to Boston with an express connection to Kings Cross. This was a popular service.

Meanwhile the goods, usually hauled by a class N5 0-6-2T or a class J11 0-6-0, would arrive at Woodhall Junction from Lincoln at about 8.00 am. At the junction it reformed its train, collecting wagons left overnight. Once the passenger train had arrived from Horncastle the goods made its way to the town, calling to marshall wagons in Woodhall Spa coal yard siding. Out-going freight had to be collected and taken to Horncastle, as the track layout at Woodhall Spa did not allow collection on the return journey.

On arrival at Horncastle the locomotive shunted wagons, often thirty or forty, before the engine was attached to the articulated twin-set in the bay platform, to form the 12.42 pm train to Woodhall Junction. This connected with a train from Lincoln to Boston and one from Skegness to Lincoln. A relief crew, driver, fireman and guard, travelled from Lincoln to replace the morning shift, who returned to Lincoln. The return to Horncastle saw the engine spending time reforming the goods wagons, before bringing the schoolchildren home on the teatime passenger train to Woodhall Junction, with connections to Boston and Lincoln. A mid-evening train from Boston and back completed the day's working.

Battle for Survival

In July 1952 the Eastern Region of the Railway Executive published a letter proposing the closure to passengers of the Woodhall Junction to Horncastle railway. It suggested that a slight modification of the timings of the Lincolnshire Road Car Company would satisfy the public need. It concluded, "as far as coal and freight traffic is concerned, there will be no alteration to our siding at Woodhall Spa station and the station yard at Horncastle will still be open to deal with traffic in full-wagon loads. Parcels and other traffic, less than wagon loads, will be dealt with by motors radiating from Woodhall Junction".

After a shaky start, during which written objections to the closure from local bodies went astray, the Railway Executive made a statement declaring no opposition to its proposals. At this point the campaign to retain passenger services began in earnest. It was orchestrated and brilliantly led by Richard Chatterton, Clerk of the Horncastle Urban Council. The Urban and Rural Councils of Horncastle, the Urban Council of Woodhall Spa, the Horncastle Chamber of Trade, the Agricultural Workers Union, the Women's Voluntary Service, the Women's Institute and Commander J. W. Maitland, put up a fierce struggle to reverse the Railway Executives proposals, a fight that lasted two years and, at one stage almost succeeded.

Class N5 0-6-2T No 69275, of Lincoln shed, at Horncastle station in July 1950. As well as working the branch these engines were used on station pilot duties at Lincoln Central station. No 69275 was built by Beyer, Peacock & Co. for the GCR in February 1894, and was withdrawn in November 1955. *M. Black.*

The Horncastle set, with "Horncastle Branch" painted above the buffer beam, at Horncastle on 12th June, 1951. The articulated coaches shared a middle bogie and were numbered E44161/2. *M. Black.*

Horncastle station with its train shed in place. An unexpected advert for the "Sheffield Telegraph" features on the end wall. *D. Thompson.*

Class C12 4-4-2T No 4016 stands with the Horncastle set in Woodhall Spa station with a service to Horncastle in 1930. *J. Wrottesley.*

Despite a gallant struggle it was announced that on Saturday 11th September, 1954, the 7.57 pm train from Horncastle would be the last passenger train to travel over the branch. Ex-Great Central Railway class 9n (LNER A5) 4-6-2T No 69803 of Boston shed was the engine designated to haul the last passenger train.

Black crepe was tied to the door handles of the carriages and Woodhall Spa provided a wreath for the front of the engine, the insignia read, "The Last Round-Up". At Horncastle station flowers were presented to driver G. H. Luff.

With an eye to business the authorities had put on a six-coach train, anticipating many a sentimental last journey. "This is the first time I've travelled on this line", was a remark passed by several passengers, and perhaps contained the whole reason why the service was being withdrawn. Relief stationmaster at Woodhall Spa was Percy Carter. Mr A. Craven, the signalman there, was transferred to Woodhall Junction, a promotion for him. Woodhall Spa people would no doubt miss his 30 or 40-yard sprint from his box to the crossing gate on Broadway.

Class A5 4-6-2T No 69803 with the last passenger train to Horncastle at Boston, driver G. H. Luff and fireman J. Marriot on the footplate, on 11th September, 1954. *S. Priestley.*

A Sheffield to Skegness unit leaves Woodhall Junction, while a class 31/1 D5878 waits for the road with a goods for Horncastle, on 11th July, 1969. *J. Vaughan.*

In the summer of 1970 a class 31 diesel works a short goods train over Thornton Crossing.

FREIGHT ONLY

After closure to passengers the branch continued to work freight, chiefly petrol, agricultural machinery, coal and tyres for agricultural vehicles. Latterly, freight was worked by diesel locomotives operated by Lincoln drivers and guards. Class 37s, class 10 and class 08 shunters were regulars on the branch.

Steve Priestly described a brake van ride on the branch in the summer of 1969: "Having cycled from Boston to Woodhall Junction, a journey of some sixteen miles, I approached the signalman who told me the Lincoln-Horncastle freight had just left Southrey, five miles to the north. The driver and guard of D3387, a Lincoln based 350 shunter, agreed to give me a ride up the branch in the brake van. After various shunting manoeuvres had been completed, and some wagons at the rear of the train collected, the signalman gave the "right away" and slowly the ten-wagon train made its way onto the branch.

Arriving at Woodhall Spa the train stopped to allow the driver to open the crossing gates. Having cleared the crossing it was the guard's duty to close the gates. There were seven gates to be opened and closed each time. Leaving Woodhall Spa the line ran through the golf course and close to the B1191 Woodhall-Horncastle road until the very narrow and overgrown Horncastle canal was reached, close by Martin Road Bridge. We followed the canal into Horncastle.

It had taken an hour to complete the journey and by this time it was raining, the only shelter in the station was the shunter's hut, there being only one part-time employee at Horncastle at this time. The freight was uncoupled and left in the small yard to be sorted and the previous days empties were collected from the siding. All point operations were done by hand as the signal box had been long since closed. With the wagons coupled up we were on our way back to Woodhall Junction where we arrived at about 4.00 pm. It was a trip I will always remember, like stepping back in time, something which, alas, can never be repeated."

After the line was finally closed on 6th April, 1971, it was eventually bought by Lincolnshire County Council, for £3,800 in 1975, and now forms part of the Viking Way. Nothing remains of the pretty Woodhall Spa station, except the row of shops in Broadway that backed up to it. The station building at Woodhall Junction survives as a private residence. At Horncastle the station lasted until 1985, when it was demolished by its owners, B. A. Bush, a tyre company.

D4075 with a brake van crosses the main road in Woodhall Spa in 1970. *D. Enefer.*

After collecting two tank wagons at Horncastle the train is ready to return over the branch and onwards to Lincoln. *D. Enefer.*

D4075 at Thornton Crossing between Woodhall Spa and Horncastle. *D. Enefer.*

The guard of the Horncastle goods closes the crossing gates near Woodhall Spa on 20th August, 1970. There is a feeling of neglect manifested by the unpainted crossing gates and overgrown trackbed. *J. Vaughan.*

The last goods train on the Horncastle branch, at Woodhall Junction on Saturday 3rd April, 1971.

The end is nigh: a run-down Horncastle station site on 11th April, 1981. *A. Cartwright.*